Career Guidance

for the High School Graduate
Want a Job in
Customer Service and Beyond?

Heartfelt Lessons to Empower YOU

YVONNE MITCHELL

authorHOUSE®

AuthorHouse™
1663 Liberty Drive
Bloomington, IN 47403
www.authorhouse.com
Phone: 833-262-8899

Published by AuthorHouse 01/04/2023

ISBN: 978-1-6655-7898-1 (sc)
ISBN: 978-1-6655-7897-4 (e)

CONTENTS

Introduction vii

What is Customer Service? 1
    Fast Growing Segment of the Job Market 3
Learn What High School Didn't Teach You 5
Extrovert vs Introvert 7
    Best Your Best You 7
    Smiling is Not a Weakness 8
Job Announcement 13
    The Employment Application 14
Job Search Resources 21
The Power of Your Smile 25
The Interview 27
    In-Person Interview 28
    Telephone Interview 29
    Virtual Interview 30
Your One-Minute Commercial 33
Interview Questions 35
Sample Interview Questions 37
Questions and Answers (Q&A) 39
Business Appearance (I Want to be Me) 43
Work Ethic 47

Socialization, Not Gossip 48

Meanness, the Snark 48

Focus on the Job 49

Telephone Voice 51

The Word Track, The Script 53

Identify Yourself 54

The Surname 54

Thank You for Calling 55

Thank You for Holding 57

Have a Great Day 58

Your Attitude 59

Politeness & Courtesy 63

Power of "Thank You" 63

No Judgment Zone 64

Self-Evaluation: You According to You 65

Conclusion 73

INTRODUCTION

S ometime ago, *I asked two impressionable teenagers, "What do you want out of life?" Their answer, "I want a future."*

Yes, you want a future. But how can you create a path towards a future of promise without knowing where to start the journey for what you want? What are the steps to take? *How do you evolve into adulthood with limited, if any, knowledge, resources and support? Is it attainable?*

The so-called "rite of passage" moment is near beginning for many teenagers to claim a space in the adult world. A scary place in the real world in which you are expected to be a productive adult, get a job, and earn your way through. These new responsibilities can sometimes come without receiving much guidance from your so-called support network, if there was one.

You may be expected to continue your education after high school by attending *a* university, community college, or trade school. *If furthering your education is not in your plans, then it is expected for you to secure a job to support yourself. If living under the roof of your guardian(s) or parent(s), you may have to move out on your own or contribute to the family budget.*

Moving on as an adult after high school with minimal skills is challenging to most. The big unknown may cloud your thinking.

"Where do I start without anyone showing me how to do it?" We all need guidance, a mentor, in our life somewhere along the way to help pave a path to a promising future.

First, you must start *by* finding a job after high school to earn money, have purchasing power. At your high school, there may not have been a class offered in career guidance. During my high school years, there were classes available to students interested in the trades, including courses and workshops in cosmetology, auto mechanics, hospitality and so on. These courses were for those who wanted to pursue a career without the benefit of college. *While trade classes are no longer taught in high school, there are now trade schools one can attend as an alternative option to college.*

I wanted to write this book on customer service as the first step for those marginalized by life's circumstances to have hope for a future. *I believe that if you don't have any other options for a career path, understanding the skillset of customer service will allow you to be employable in any business and industry.* It is a skill that employers need to sustain and grow their businesses.

Customer service has a place in the majority of businesses. If you have *little or no* work experience, a customer service job may be the best place to start your employment experience.

There are such companies still around that do consider applicants with *little to no* work experience. For a future employer to hire you, solely based on your potential and character, you need to show a willingness to be trained on the job, *understand the mindset of customer service and accept direction/instruction* with a positive can-do/will-try attitude.

To be a successful customer service employee in any industry and business means assuming good behavioral assets and understanding communication with others. Identify "improvement needed" in behavior and communication. Exercise intentional improvement and personal growth mindset on your journey to a job and life with promise.

To help grow my small business in sales, I intentionally hired customer service representatives who lacked experience in effort to teach them the customer service skillset. I wanted them to be the most effective and qualified customer service applicant should they move on to other job opportunities outside of my business. My employees understood that with an open mind and acceptance of new knowledge they would benefit from having a new skillset to build upon for the future.

The entry level customer service job is a first step, not the end-all. There will be many more opportunities to grow your career once mastering this essential skillset. Additionally, it is advisable to take on further education by attending a university, college, community college, or trade school to grow your future.

Proceed in life with a vision to keep moving forward and upward in your chosen journey. Educate yourself!

This guidebook will provide information (probably not taught during your high school years) that is necessary to landing your first customer service job. Entry level customer service jobs are plentiful, available and a good way to earn a living straight out of high school. This guidebook will provide insights on the application process, interview and as a hired customer service employee, as well as continuing your path to self-discovery. By the time you're done with this book, you will know how to:

- Meet the challenges of the job search and office protocols.
- What is expected when working with the public.
- Communicating with customers and team members – knowing what to say, when to say and how.

If you are already working in customer service, this book will enhance your career and possibly reveal bad habits which may be blocking that promotion you so want.

We all need a chance and opportunity to be employed, earn a living and have someone believe in us. However, it's up to you to make yourself available. It's up to you to be seen. It's up to you to apply for that position and give that hiring manager a reason to believe in you. It's up to you to prove yourself worthy of being employed. This guidebook is to help you do that. Let's go!

CUSTOMER SERVICE AND YOU

WHAT IS CUSTOMER SERVICE?

*C*ustomer service means servicing the customer. It is an essential and valued position within most employing companies.

Customer service is a people-purpose job. The main function is to engage with customers ensuring satisfactory transactions and experiences on behalf of the employer. Also, having the responsibility to resolve, with accuracy and efficiency, emerging problems/concerns customers may face. In many ways, customer service employees are the first and last friendly face/voice that customers encounter for a business. The quality level of the customer service experience is key to keeping or losing customers.

Word of mouth is the best and can be the worst form of advertisement. The profitability of a business also depends on the type of service the customer receives after the business transaction. If the customer service is bad, the employer's business may be impacted by loss of customers and profits. If the customer service is good, the employer can count on a growing business with high retention. It's safe to say that customer service is the lifeblood of any company.

Small and large businesses expect to have a successful, growing business with minimal disruption. It costs them lots of money to employ sales teams to bring in business. Yet, they depend on the support of dedicated and committed customer service employees,

1

as well as a well-managed customer service department to speak on their behalf. Businesses rely on the customer service department to retain customers so that the business can continue to grow and increase revenue.

Customers want answers, not excuses, solutions, not more problems. This is why a good customer service team is a crucial part of any business. When a customer calls or emails their inquiry or complaint, it is sent to the customer service response center. It's up to the customer service agent taking the call or answering the email to address the customer's concerns in a respectfully informed manner. Customers want and need to hear pleasantries or at the very least, a helpful tone on the other end of the *telephone* line, along with an assurance that their concern or inquiry will be taken care of in an efficient way. This same rule of thumb goes for emailed inquiries and concerns. A pleasantly typed reply is reassuring and comforting. The wrong tone or inefficiency on the phone or in an email can send the customer to the competitor.

Leadership is just as important. Leadership must have the "customer first" mindset if the company expects the frontline customer service employee to represent their business in the best way. It has to start from the top of the chain of command. The customer service employee cannot do their job well without the support of leadership. An effective customer service manager and department insulates the business, minimizes customer attrition and maintains customer loyalty.

It's always great when customers give positive feedback regarding a company's customer service. When that happens, it's guaranteed the customer will return and bring other customers along. Because customer service has been taken for granted in recent times, it's nice when a customer says, "Thank you for good service." That also means customer service.

The customer service position as a start-up career choice can be learned. It's a trainable job requiring little to no experience. It is not an exact science. It is essentially behavioral skills applied to specific business practices. A common-sense thinking, empathetic position for the applicant willing to conform, possess a good work ethic and meets the expectations and requirements of the employer.

Fast Growing Segment of the Job Market

There are a wide range of customer service positions ready to be filled *with growth potential*. The description below is a generic entry level description for multiple customer service positions:

> Interact with customers to handle complaints, process orders and provide information about the company's products and services.
>
> Answer questions and requests from customer or the public.
>
> Entry Level- High school diploma or equivalent. **Note**: Higher levels of education may be desired but not required, depending on duties and responsibilities of the customer service job.

While "Customer Service" is the universal term used, there are many positions that fall under the customer service umbrella:

- Receptionist
- Cashier
- Office Clerk

- Technical Support Representative
- Call Center Representative
- Flight Attendant
- Patient Coordinator
- Help Desk Customer Representative
- Salesclerk
- Medical Office Assistant
- … and countless more.

Many more job listings are identified through job search engines such as Indeed and LinkedIn. I have found that many companies are going back to print advertising in search of applicants to fill their open positions. That being said, don't ignore your local newspaper's classified ad section.

LEARN WHAT HIGH SCHOOL DIDN'T TEACH YOU

Graduating from high school does not mean that you were sufficiently educated to secure a job to support your adult life. When all the celebrations are over and it is time to think about life after high school, primarily how to earn a living, pay rent, feed yourself and other adult essentials, you start thinking about your skills and limitations when applying for jobs. It's not easy applying for a job in today's multi-tiered application process. It takes a willfully determined person to push through the walls created to screen applicants, yet it can be done! You can successfully navigate through the maze of the job search engines and applications.

Should you come from a school system not focused on student achievement, self-educate yourself. Do yourself a favor and conduct a truly inward self-evaluation of what is required to improve your reading, writing, grammar and math. These are the basics needed to work in customer service and any other job. Enroll in remedial reading, writing or math classes at your community college, if necessary. Find a tutor to help you. If you have challenges with reading or writing, it is very difficult to complete an application and follow directions. Sacrifice social time for productive time. Invest in yourself.

Reading is the most essential skill of all the required skills to be successful in any job. It is a fundamental requirement. Next is counting and writing. You do not have to be an expert reader, writer, or counter. However, you must have acceptable, passable skills in these areas to function in a job setting.

Decoding the language is essential to reading what comes across on a computer monitor. Educating self is for those who see and want a promising future and have a vision for a better life. Do not get stuck in the setbacks of the past and hurdles of the moment. Your future opportunities are there for you to claim. Put in the time and effort on improving yourself to secure a job, a career and a future.

EXTROVERT VS INTROVERT

Having an extroverted or introverted personality should not have an impact on how well you will perform your job duties. In my experience, how you perform is more about your work ethic and skills. I have hired introverted and extroverted applicants over the years and found there is room for both in customer service.

Whether you are an extrovert or introvert, as long as you:

- Remain positive
- Get along with co-workers and supervisors
- Perform your duties and responsibilities with due-diligence and competency
- Possess a strong work ethic and calmness while performing your duties

    … you can do the job of customer service and be successful!

Best Your Best You

We are the product of our upbringing; the good, bad and ugly of it all. The cultural environments also help shape adult personalities. This dynamic determines your outlook on life as you grow into adulthood, particularly as you pursue employment to support yourself. The willingness to change for the better is the ingredient to maturity, forward thinking and self-sufficiency.

Childhood experiences are embedded in our mindset and can impact our development knowingly and unknowingly. The predisposition of harboring defensiveness, the chip on the shoulder and thoughts that someone is always out to get you can take on a personality cult of its own. The mindset of continuous negative seeps into your spirit like a runaway virus reaping havoc on your ability to communicate. It hampers your ability to extend social courtesy and kindness to others, even if you actually want to be courteous and kind. It is a wall that can block so much good in your life as well as job opportunities.

You must work on you to combat this. It will take effort and strength of mindfulness to improve your behavioral aptitude, toss negative thoughts in the trash bin and be more positive thinking. Working on this and doing these things will allow you to be your best you!

Smiling is Not a Weakness

A customer service job is about the business of reconciling customer concerns and problems. In customer service, smiling can expedite the resolution of a question or problem amicably. It can easily assist in getting the customer to accept and trust you when providing answers to their issues. Because of this, it is best to have a smiling nature than a frowning nature. You can also try a neutrally relaxed facial expression if smiling isn't warranted.

Smiling is generally defined as a facial expression. That is a simplistic definition of smiling that does not reveal the true meaning and implications of a smile. Smiling is good for releasing stress in our everyday lives, particularly in a job setting. A smile can be the ice-breaker when meeting co-workers, customers and new people, by revealing you are open to engagement. Smiling is inviting. Smiling puts people at ease and reveals the softer side of a person. Smiling also breaks communication barriers and preconceived judgments. Smiling is not a weakness. Smiling is a strength and indicates character.

Smiling is good for your appearance, mind and career. A smile can be felt through the voice over the telephone. When you smile, the customer can sense a smile as you talk. As a customer service employee, it's part of your job to be pleasant and business-like over the phone when conducting customer service calls. Whether the customer is face-to-face or over the phone, smiling is not a weakness and enhances the interaction. It's good practice to smile before answering the telephone or greeting the customer.

Smile in your everyday life. No one wants to be around a sour person, always frowning. Frowning is negative and will not help you win customers or co-workers. Frowning can be the barrier to that job or promotion you want. Frowns make others feel as if you are an angry person with hostilities waiting to strike. Don't get your face sculpted into a frown. Once it is sculpted, it is hard to reverse the frown lines on your face. Frowns pull you down and can destroy professional and personal relationships. Getting along goes a long way with an authentic smile that portrays an approachable and calming disposition.

Try to smile even if it hurts. Remember, it's not a weakness. It's a strength! Smiling is something you control and often times it is infectious. Make it a practice to smile and feel the difference in your spirit.

APPLYING FOR THE POSITION

JOB ANNOUNCEMENT

Job announcements in years past were written based on a clear understanding of what the job's duties and responsibilities involved. The entry level jobs were just that, entry level, requiring minimal experience. The ability to be trained and work well with others, essentially were the dominant qualifications. For the most part, *entry level jobs were filled with high school graduates.*

A customer service job posting would look like this:

> Looking for CSR (Customer Service Representative) for busy general office. Must be a self-starter, ability to communicate effectively. Telephone skills a must. Ability to work independently. Experience with computer keyboard required. Type 45 wpm (words per minute).

Job announcements were published in newspapers, on boards at colleges, recruiting sites, non-profits specializing in finding jobs for the unemployed or specific demographics. With the introduction of the internet, the primary portal for submitting a resume or application is through the multi-tiered job application platforms. Where your application lands when submitted through the application portal is the great unknown. You may receive a response, or you may not. Keep applying!

There are four essential components to a job announcement:

- Job Description
- Job Duties and Responsibilities
- Job Requirements and Qualifications
- Education Requirements

When reviewing a job announcement, search for key words that apply to your work or life experiences. List them on a separate page when preparing your job application and in a designated section on your resume. This is also helpful for the interview process. Life experiences like babysitting, volunteering within your community, assistant teachers, etc., should not be discounted. Employers will look at this as experience in communication, working well with others and character references.

The point is to not be discouraged due to lacking in work experience. You'd be amazed how far something like babysitting experience can take you in the customer service job market.

The Employment Application

Applications are essentially completed online through a myriad of job search sites or through the remaining brick and mortar employment agencies. Very seldom can you walk into a business and ask for a paper application these days. The sign in the window of a business may say, "We are hiring," yet the application is more than likely accessed through the company's website or a third-party job search portal.

Once you've completed the application, you may hear back from the company or job recruitment site, or you may not. Don't let that discourage your job search. Keep applying and using key words from the job announcement. Because of the filters and algorithms within these website portals, key words can be your friend or your nemesis. The algorithms and filters are designed to reject applications without key words and accept applications with key words. If you're unsure, have someone with experience look over your application/resume for errors and key words/phrases before submitting. You may have to revise to improve your chances. If so, this is a good thing. It means you are advancing towards your goal.

The format of the application is standard, for the most part. Specific information will be required whether the application is paper, or computer generated. The important lesson is to be prepared to answer with the requested information in an accurate and logical manner. Be consistent when completing applications.

QUICK TIP: To save yourself some time and for future reference when completing applications, have a downloaded copy of a completed application or resume. Refer to either as you complete a new application for a new company or position.

Here is how to answer fields of information on a generic application:

PERSONAL INFORMATION

- Date of Application – The date you completed the application
- Last Name, then First Name
- Middle Name – If you have a middle name, it's important to at least include the initial to avoid being confused with another

applicant of the same name. You don't want to be denied an opportunity due to misidentification.

- Address – Many companies are removing this field to avoid prejudicial and discriminatory claims. In lieu of this, companies may ask for your zip code only in efforts to hire applicants living close to the business. Employers don't want employees tardy/absent due to "traffic" or "distance." For the companies still using this field, you can choose to use your mailing address or current home address.

EMPLOYMENT INFORMATION

- Position Desired/Applying For – Use the title in the job announcement
- Start Date – Use a present date or ASAP (As Soon As Possible)
- Salary Desired – Use the salary on the job announcement or write "Open" to give you and the employer flexibility in setting a wage based on the level of experience.
- Are You Currently Employed? – Tell the truth, yes or no.
- If So, May We Contact Your Employer? – If you are currently employed, say "Yes," or leave blank until you are confident that this is the job for you. This question can be raised again during the interview, when you will have a better understanding of the position.
- Have You Applied to This Company Before? If Yes, Please Indicate Where and When? – Be honest. List the truthful answers to this question.
- Have You Worked for This Company Before?

  If Yes, Please Indicate Your Position and When – If yes, save the explanation for the interview.

- Do You Seek Full or Part-Time Employment? – Indicate which one. Part-time in California is less than 40 hours per week, according to the California Labor Code, section 515(c).

  Full-time is 30 hours or more per week, according to IRS.com.

- Shift or Hours Preferred? – Open. It's best not to indicate a specific shift or hours until you are more into the interview. If pressed, say that you are flexible. If not flexible, state which hours you can actually work. You must be honest with yourself and to this process.

- Do You Have Special Skills, Experience, or Qualifications Relating to the Position? – Here is where you reference the skills/experience/key words list mentioned in the *Job Announcement* section of this book – "... search for key words that apply to your work or life experiences. List them on a separate page ..." Use the job description as a guide to help define your skills, experience, or qualifications. Mirror the job description and desired qualifications of the job announcement that apply. These are your key words to help get past the pesky algorithms.

- Do You Have Any Physical Limitations Which Would Hinder Your Performance in the Position Applied For? – Many companies are removing this question to avoid bias and discriminatory claims. For companies still asking, honestly answer. The American Disabilities Act protects employees as well as future applicants from discrimination.

EMPLOYMENT HISTORY

- List Previous Employers & Dates of Employment – If you are working at the time of completing an application, start with your current employer and list in descending date order, from current to first. The time frame should cover no more than a 10-year span.

- Earnings History – Most entry level positions do not have negotiated pay ranges. The pay is based on a preset schedule sanctioned by the employer. If this is your first job, just write "N/A" and move forward.

  If you have a salary history, I suggest leaving salary history blank. It is a way for new employers to gauge what they can offer you based on your previous employment salary. Do salary research on the company and position using Google. Prepare to answer the salary question with an informed answer.

- May We Contact Your Current Employer? – If you are currently working, this can be left blank until the job you are applying for is offered. However, if pressed, answer yes or no. Beware! Answering this question can be a two-edged sword. If you don't want your current employer to know you are seeking new employment, answer no and let the chips fall where they may.

- Title, Duties and Reason for Leaving – If you've never had a job, this is where you list relevant skills, experience and qualifications acquired from babysitting, volunteering and assisting. Honesty is still the best policy. When you make it to the interview, explain that this will be your first job and why they should hire you.

  For the employed, be prepared to log at least one year of prior work experience. Use titles from the company's Human Resources' department. List duties in a quantitative way. Give reasons for any lapse of time between jobs. If there is no room on the application, be sure to discuss duties and lapse of time during the interview. The interviewer will inquire.

The reason for leaving can be tricky. Keep the reasons positive and non-monetary. Avoid negative comments about previous companies, co-workers, or management. Look into the light, not the dark of your employment experiences. A positive example: "I want a more challenging position to utilize other skills I possess."

- Special Skills/Knowledge – This is where you list relevant computer skills (hardware and software applications), typing speed, telephone systems, certifications received, etc. Whatever you think will help you stand out from the other applicants. An example: Other applicants may only know Excel, while you know Microsoft 365. List it!

EDUCATION

Whether it's high school, college, or a technical school, the questions are self-explanatory and the same. Be prepared to give:
- o   Name of institution
- o   Address o Dates of attendance o Did you graduate?
- o   Degree level (if higher than high school)

REFERENCES

Some companies will not request references, and some will, especially if you have no work history. In this case, give names and phone numbers of individuals you can be assured will provide a clear and positive reference for you.

If you volunteered at a center, use the person's name that gave you instruction. If you babysat, use the parents' name of the child(ren). If you assisted a teacher, use the teacher. It's also ok to use your best friend's parent if they like you.

In any case, before listing reference, it is important to first obtain the reference's permission. Never list a reference without their permission. It is unprofessional and may not work in your favor.

After your application is reviewed by the screener or recruiter, you may be contacted by phone, email, or text for an interview. The next section will prepare for both face-to-face and over-the-phone interviews.

JOB SEARCH RESOURCES

Now that you know how to apply for the job, you need to know where to apply. Here is a list of online employment agencies and resources to help you get started in your search.

It is perfectly acceptable and normal to apply to them all.

www.glassdoor.com

www.google.com

www.indeed.com

www.linkedin.com

Robert Half
Talent Solutions

www.roberthalf.com

SimplyHired.

www.simplyhired.com

ZipRecruiter

www.ziprecruiter.com

Keep reading to learn how to master the interview, get hired and stay employed.

PREPARING FOR THE INTERVIEW & POSITION

THE POWER OF YOUR SMILE

Remember, as previously stated in the *Customer Service and You* section, "Smiling is NOT a weakness!" Smiling exudes confidence. Even if your confidence may be lacking, a smile gives the impression that your confidence is intact. This is a trait you want to shine during your interview.

In interviews with potential employers, "Smile for the cameras," as the saying goes. Smiling relaxes the interviewer and shows that you possess a caring, humble nature and a willingness to get along with others should you get the job. Everyone has the capacity to smile and with a great smile, it places us all on the same page when looking for a commonality in relationships.

If the interviewer doesn't smile face-to-face or over the phone, that's ok. This is the one time you do not want to mirror the other. In either case, don't lose the power of your smile. Keep smiling or take a neutral calm expression. Think smiling thoughts. Whether on the phone or face-to-face, the interviewer will pick-up on your calmness and confidence.

THE INTERVIEW

The application along with the interview are both vetting processes. Companies are taking big chances with each new hire. It is important applicants take the application and interview as serious as possible because their futures depend on it.

Due to the pandemic of 2020, an increase in remote work and a demand for work-life balance, face-to-face or in-person interviews have become less and less the norm. Virtual (online, video conferencing) interviews have taken center-stage over in-person and telephone interviews. However, some companies prefer that personal touch. Also, depending on the job itself, an in-person interview may be necessary.

Certain characteristics must be adhered to in all interview types. Whether it's a virtual, in-person, or telephone interview, the interviewer is paying close attention to your:

- Character – The way you think, feel and behave – Stay positive!
- Maturity – The wisdom displayed through conversation
- Mannerisms/Movement – The way you carry yourself (walk, talk, sit).

Improving your interview skills should be an ongoing process. How you interview for your first job, should not be how you interview for your second, third, and so on. The best way to improve your interview skills:

- Rehearse your verbal responses – Summarize your work/ volunteer/assisting background, desire to work with the company, your personal strengths and your best subject in school.

It's also important to be conscious of these specific factors. The interviewer looks for:

- Ability – Convince them that you are able to do the job and do it with confidence.
- Personality – Remember the *Power of Your Smile* whether you are on the phone, in-person or virtual.

These notes of observation may be subjective. It's best to stay positive to counter any adverse judgments you may not have control over. Example: A millennial may be interviewed by a baby boomer. The millennial must stay positive just in case this particular baby boomer has not accepted society's evolvement. It happens. Don't let that discourage you. Prove to them, you are worthy, you are capable, and you belong!

The above accounts for all types of interviews. Now, let's breakdown specifics to add based on the type of interview.

In-Person Interview

Along with the aforementioned, appearance is a big factor with in-person interviews. Interviewers look for neatness:

- Well-groomed hair – Pop culture styles may deter the interviewer. Try a wig if your hair is in a permanent pop culture style.
- Well-presented face – Clean shaven or well-applied makeup
- Clean nails – If manicures are not your thing, clean under the nails
- Good body odor – Perfumes and colognes can be overbearing. Some people may be allergic. Shower with soap and water and use a neutral lotion. Apply perfumes/colognes after the interview.

Be practical with your appearance. You want a job not to win a popularity contest. There is room for individuality, yet don't go overboard.

Telephone Interview

When it comes to telephone interviews, there is less to consider. However, there are still items to include along with the previously mentioned like:

- Connection – You never want the call to accidentally disconnect during a telephone interview. If using a cell phone, be sure you're not in a drop-zone/dead-zone area. If using a landline, be sure the bill is paid prior to the call.
- Surroundings – Ensure the surroundings are quiet. Noises can distract you and the interviewer.
- Smiling – Remember the *Power of Your Smile*. The interviewer can hear if you are smiling while on the phone!

- Interruptions – If using a cell phone, change the notification sounds to silent or vibrate.

  You don't want a loud text message notification to sound-off during your interview.

Remember this is a business call, which requires business etiquette. Treat it as such.

Virtual Interview

Here's a list of what to consider when preparing for your virtual interview on top of the previous interview checklist:

- Physical Environment
  - o Location – Quiet with little to no distractions.
  - o Lighting – Make sure the room is well-lit. An inexpensive desk or sitting near a window with the curtains pulled back will suffice.
  - o Surroundings – Remember, the interviewer can see your immediate surroundings. Some virtual platforms allow you to hide your background. Prepare as if that is not the case. Your surroundings should be clean and organized with a glass or bottle of water. Your virtual interview background should mimic an in-person interview background.

- Technology
  - o Internet Connection – The worst thing for your video to constantly stop or disconnect during a virtual interview. Test your internet speed. If it's too slow, go to your local

library or a friend/family member's home to have your virtual interview.

o Video Software – Your interviewer will send you a link for the interview. This will let you know which video platform you will be using. Download it and test it before the interview. Play with the settings and become familiar. It's unprofessional to come to a virtual interview ill-prepared with the video software.

o Audio/Video – Testing the video software's settings includes testing the microphone and *camera*. Be sure your camera is clean! Be sure your camera works. It's best to wear a headset with a microphone as it will improve the quality of your voice.

YOUR ONE-MINUTE COMMERCIAL

*Y*our one-minute commercial is a to-the-point, rehearsed summation of your prior experience and qualifications. In the previous section, we mentioned, "Rehearse your verbal responses." Your verbal responses are paired with your one-minute commercial. When asked by the interviewer to express, in your own words, why you are qualified for the position, your one-minute commercial is your response.

Picture yourself as a product you are marketing to the interviewer, as companies market products to us through commercials. In essence, you are marketing the work you will do for that company as a commodity, a product. If hired, that company will pay you for your work, your commodity, your product. If your work suffers and causes the company grief, the company will decide to no longer pay you for your work, your commodity, your product, i.e., termination.

Reflect and conduct an inventory of your life experiences including babysitting, volunteering in the community, helping at a relative's or friend's business and education that fits with the job description and qualifications. Mirror the job description as much as possible. Relevancy of requirements is very important. Remember key words and phrases to pull from the job announcement that match your prior experiences. Write/type your lists and you are ready to create your commercial.

Start your one-minute commercial with how you know you are qualified for the job and a good hire. Incorporate your work history and life experiences lists and how they relate to the specific job. End your one-minute commercial by emphasizing your ease in grasping new concepts and willingness to be trained in new areas. This is your one-minute commercial.

It needs to be delivered with ease and again, confidence. Practice and rehearse as much as possible. Perform in front of an honest friend or record yourself using your cell phone. Playback the videos to see where you need to improve. You can learn a lot about yourself when you record yourself and watch the playback.

INTERVIEW QUESTIONS

Here's another *confidence-building* practice. *To help prepare you for your first or promoted customer service position, I want you to get in the habit of knowing how it feels to be interviewed for an opportunity. The best way to do that is through action!*

The next few pages are a sampling of routine interview questions. Grab a pen and pad. I want you to write down the answers and responses as best you can. Be honest. You may have to think each one through before answering. In doing so, I want you to pull from your life experiences and past work history to answer each question. Your answers will show the interviewer you are capable *and ready to hire.*

Before you move forward, Google and research the company. Read their "About" page and "Mission Statement" found on their individual website. Familiarize yourself with their products, career opportunities and if possible, pay scale. You want to know the overall character of the company and have a good understanding of the position in which you have applied. Speak to the language of the job announcement as it is your easiest and best reference.

Please note, some of these questions were asked on the application. It's possible your application was reviewed and accepted by someone else, and the interviewer is unaware of your answers. Don't be discouraged with redundancy.

If you've never had a job, inform the interviewer. They will adjust their *questioning to suit your possible life experiences and volunteer history. Once this happens, you can answer many of the* job-related questions by *splitting* up *Your One-Minute Commercial* based on the specific question.

SAMPLE INTERVIEW QUESTIONS

Often times, the questions are set-up in a particular order. Sometimes, they are scattered about to show how quickly the interviewee (applicant) can adjust.

Whether the job is retail, call center, hospitality, administrative, etc., these routine questions will be asked among others:

1. What do you know about our company and services/products?
2. Why do you want to work for our company?
3. What does "customer service" mean to you?
4. Are you able to type 40 words per minute?
5. What computer hardware and software programs are most proficient?
6. Describe a customer service experience you resolved to the customer's satisfaction.
7. How would you resolve a customer's concern in which you have limited knowledge?
8. What does "detail oriented" mean to you?
9. Tell me a time when you dealt with a difficult customer or situation. How did you resolve the issue? Was a supervisor, teacher, or mentor called for guidance and assistance?
10. Do you consider yourself a positive person? Why?

11. Do you feel you work best alone or in a group? Are you a loner or team player?

12. Are you willing to be trained and work under direct supervision?

13. If hired, what are your short-term goals with the company?

14. What two words would your family and friends use to describe you?

15. Would anyone describe you as dependable? If so, who?

16. Based on your experience, what duties or responsibilities did you enjoy most and least? Why?

17. How do you feel about doing repetitive work?

18. Are you a problem-solver? Give me an example of when you successfully solved a problem satisfying all parties involved. (not the same as # 9)

19. How would you respond to an angry, argumentative, or verbally abusive customer?

20. What additional information should I know about you? Why should we hire you?

A good idea would be to create a one-minute commercial for each question above. You don't want to be repetitive nor long-winded, yet you do want to be thorough.

If your one-minute commercial answers all of these questions as is, you're doing good. The interviewer *will screen many applicants and it's important that* you stand out amongst the list.

You want to be remembered. You want to leave a positive mark, and good impression in the interviewer's memory.

Be disciplined with your answers by keeping them short and relevant, unless asked to elaborate.

Remember to smile!

QUESTIONS AND ANSWERS (Q&A)

I thought it would be helpful to give you some sample answers, so you'd have a better idea at what the interviewers are looking for in your responses.

1. How would you deal with an angry customer?

    I would listen carefully to their concerns/complaints. From there, I would show empathy and follow company policy. I would also remain positive and proactive in an understanding and patient way. I won't take anything personally as I try to resolve their concern at my level. If I'm unable, I will place the customer on a brief hold (if on the phone) and reach out to a supervisor for additional support. If in person, I would inform the customer and excuse myself to go find a supervisor for additional support.

2. Give me an example of time you went to great lengths to help a customer or person.

    If you've never had a job, again, pull from past life experiences.
    Example: Tell when a parent thought they lost their child and you, being the favorite babysitter, volunteered to help.

The child woke-up from their nap scared, due to a bad dream. When she awoke, she ran to her favorite hiding place. I found the child because when I babysit, I interact with the child. I don't just watch tv and talk on the phone. I perform the job at hand. I don't take its ease for granted.

3. Why should we hire you?

    I am a hard worker, willing to go the extra mile to complete my task. I believe in arriving to work on time, ready to work and earning my pay. I have good work ethic because at the end of the day, I need to know I put my best foot forward. I am willing to be trained and eager to learn new skills.

4. How well do you work under pressure in high stress situations?

    If you've never had to work in these conditions, explain how you think you would manage.

    I'm a level-headed person and believe I am able to keep calm during situations where a customer is not satisfied with any of my responses or attempts of resolve. I will not take it personally. I understand stressful times are apparent. It's been said displaying a calm tone, results in calm tones from all parties. I will continue to work with the customer, displaying a calm tone and patience. If nothing works, I will refer the customer to my supervisor and inform my supervisor of the issue at hand.

5. Can you work with others as a member of the team in your department?

    Yes. I am a team player. I believe in team harmony and participation. I understand it takes team effort and coordination to meet the duties and responsibilities of the department as a whole.

WORKING THE POSITION

BUSINESS APPEARANCE (I WANT TO BE ME)

CONGRATULATIONS!!! You got the job!! You signed the paperwork!! You know where you will go and the date and time to be there!! But wait! What are you going to wear?

We all want to be and express ourselves as often as possible. I often dreamed of being myself, dressing in long bohemian skirts and blouses with sandalled feet and growing my hair wild. Freedom to be me! The problem with this, it wasn't allowed in the workplace during my career building years, and it's still not necessarily allowed now. In the business world, I had to dress either formally or business casual, which is different from casual.

It is the company's responsibility to give you a new employee packet either prior to starting work or on your first day. It is YOUR responsibility to inquire about the dress code. Yes, take initiative and simply ask, "Is there a specific dress code?"

The answer may be, "business casual," or "there's no dress code," or something else. Again, it's YOUR responsibility to find out. If you don't know what the dress code is on day one, it is best practice to dress in business casual. Let me explain what that is.

Business casual is a neat appearance mixing formal business attire and casual attire. Most businesses flocked to business casual over the years. Few are casual as society has evolved somewhat. As a customer service employee, business casual is usually the norm.

Unless your new customer service position is an industry with a uniform, like a restaurant, hospital, hotel, etc., there is somewhat of a uniform for business casual. According to Indeed.com ...

Options for Women:

- Knee-length skirts/dresses
- Slacks/khaki pants
- Blouses, sweaters, button-downs, polo shirts (never sleeveless)
- Maxi skirts/maxi dresses
- Optional cardigans, blazers, or jackets
- Closed-toed shoes like flats, boots, loafers, heels
- Simplistic jewelry, belts, accessories.

Options for Men:

- Button-down shirts, sweaters or polo shirts
- Closed-toed shoes such as loafers
- Optional belt that matches your shoes
- Optional tie and jacket or sport coat

Options for Gender-neutral:

- Slacks, khakis or other non-denim pants
- A Sweater
- A button-down shirt or something tidy-looking
- Boots or loafers

Casual Fridays can be tricky since different businesses have different dress codes. Always consult with your supervisor or employee handbook as to what is and is not acceptable for Casual Fridays. Classic fit jeans without holes might be acceptable.

Be prepared to be a serious player in the real world of employment. Career building is more than what you know and what you do. It's also how you represent the company and how you present yourself to your employer and peers. Pop culture styles and images are not proper work attire unless the company has adapted that into their corporate culture. Until you know this for certain, stay away from it. Business casual is always the best way to start!

WORK ETHIC

Employers expect new hires to comply with their protocols, procedures and culture of the company. They expect *Your One-Minute Commercial* to show up and back its promises. The employer wants an employee with a good work ethic mentality.

Having good work ethic essentially means to arrive to work on time, according to the work schedule, and perform the duties and responsibilities assigned, as defined by your job title.

It is not good practice to call in sick because you don't want to get up the morning after staying out late the night before. That is bad work ethic. You don't want to call in sick because of personal, relationship issues. In either case, good work ethic means you plan ahead and accordingly. If you went out the night before, you go home at a decent hour because you know you must attend work the next day. If you are having relationship issues, you shake it off until after the workday has ended. It is YOUR responsibility to go to work and be on time. You gave this company your word that you would be the best employee. They trusted your word, so now you must show up and prove that you were worth the hire.

Socialization, Not Gossip

Socialization skills are a requisite for pursuing a job in any field, especially, customer service. Positive socialization engagement with your co-workers allows you to gain more knowledge from them that may be helpful to your bank of knowledge and your career. Practice positive socialization communication on the job. It will benefit you immediately and in the long run.

The lines between socialization and gossip can be blurred only if you aren't paying attention. Socialization is not gossiping about your co-workers' personal issues or informing your co-workers of your own personal issues. That is a no-no. It's best to keep personal conversations to a minimum as much as possible. Too much personal conversations will turn into gossip and interfere with your ability to complete your job.

Gossip creates tension and the office gossip circuit is toxic. Office gossip has been known to destroy careers, productivity and the overall positive nature of the office environment.

Some people tend not to interact with co-workers for fear of the gossiping affects. This lack of inability to communicate with co-workers disrupts your ability to work with them and share work information. If you keep your conversations to work-related topics, this lack of interaction can turn into a positive co-working experience.

Meanness, the Snark

Meanness, the snark may be popular and a selling feature on social media. Outside of social media, when pursuing a career in the working world, meanness, the snark is not an attractive personality trait.

You must get along with people. There's an old phrase, "No man is an island," meaning one can't do everything on their own. Express a positive, purposeful demeanor on your job in customer service and everyday life. The snark in you creates an atmosphere of tension in your workplace and may lead to frustration in your engagements with your colleagues and employers. Stay positive.

There will be times when you have given your all and communications may not be going in a positive direction. Shake that off and stay focused on your behavior. You can not change others behavior towards you if they have meanness, the snark in them. Shake off hostile, defensive demeanors and resume a positive disposition. Rise above where others are trying to take you. Stay the course, be positive in your communications and interactions and take on a purposeful attitude. Remember to *Be Your Best You*!

Focus on the Job

A workday means a day of performing duties and tasks assigned to you by your supervisor to meet the goals and needs of the company. Whether it's your first day or 100th day, come to work ready to focus on the job, as assigned. When you come to work and clock in, you are no longer on your time. You are on the company's time, the employer's payroll. You must be attentive to the job at hand and not your personal issues/business. Make a concerted effort to free your mind of the personal distractions.

The cell phone is the biggest distraction in the workplace. To remain focused while at work, you must limit your cell phone use. Ways to limit cell phone usage:

- Turn the ringer to silent or vibrate.
- Set firm instructions with family and friends as to when they can and should contact you during work hours.

- Be disciplined and use your phone during lunch and 15 minute- breaks, not restroom runs.
- If an emergency arises, inform your supervisor before acting
- Even if your employer has a social media page, stay off social media until you are off-the-clock.

You will be observed by your supervisor, especially as a new hire. The less distractions to have, the better your work ethic will be and appear to management.

TELEPHONE VOICE

Many customer service positions are remote or in a call-center, which means they are telephone positions. Your set-up consists of a computer, a headset, and a telephone you are connected to for the majority of your workday. If you're in a call-center, you have a cubicle area. If you're remote, your set-up is your own.

As a telephone, customer service employee, your tone of voice, known as your Telephone Voice, is as important to your job as the telephone itself.

You represent the company. It's your responsibility to maintain a professional, calming tone and manner when speaking with a customer. Remember the *Power of Your Smile*, because without it, over-the-phone, customers can sense and hear:

- Tiredness
- Frustration
- Hurried rush to complete the call

If a customer senses and hears any of the aforementioned, they will not feel as if their needs or concerns are being addressed or met. If you have an irate customer, this can increase their anger and prompt dissatisfaction. Dissatisfied customers complain to supervisors and leave businesses for their competitors. You don't want this to happen because you:

- Rushed the caller.
- Made them feel ignored.
- Allowed your tone to be less than empathetic and concerning.

Your tone of voice can impede your ability to reconcile the customer's concern or problem. Work on your telephone voice. Drink warm, decaffeinated tea at the start of your day and room temperature water throughout the day. This will help the larynx and decrease possible workday stresses.

THE WORD TRACK, THE SCRIPT

The business language of customer service is essentially the same no matter the industry. Uniform phrasing referred to as the word track or script should be followed. The employer expects the employee to know how to communicate with the customer using their company approved word track/script.

Most fast-food restaurants with drive thru or telephone orders, call-centers and some office settings use a word track/script. The word track/script is a roadmap to answer general inquiries and leading to resolutions of various complaints and concerns that may arise from a customer call. *Follow it!* It will direct you where to find answers and can help with communicating in a strategic manner.

The basic word track/script consists of the same sections:

- Identifying Yourself
- The Surname
- Thank You for Calling
- Thank You for Holding
- Have a Great Day

Identify Yourself

Customers want to know who they are speaking with when they call a business. More often than not, customers write down the name of the person they spoke to for future reference.

Many companies have protocols in place for their employees' identification during a call. This is so the company can secure their employees and track the call. Identification assignments can be an alias name, alpha numeric signature, or allowing you to use your first or last name. It varies by company. Either way, you will be instructed how to identify yourself on the customer call.

It's best practice to identify yourself immediately, prior to learning of the customer's reason for calling. Be clear with your identification. You don't want the customer to ask you to repeat it. Also, if your call is being monitored, your supervisor will want to know you clearly identified yourself.

The Surname

In our more casual society, we tend to treat everyone as a familiar acquaintance. This should not be the case in a business setting while working in customer service. It is always best practice to address a customer over-the-phone by their surname. The surname is the last name. It is a level of respect given to the call, to address them as Mr. or Ms. Surname.

Times have changed so if you address the caller as Mr. and they correct you and say, Ms. (or vice versa) it's ok. Apologize, acknowledge the change, make notes on their file for the next customer service representative and move forward with the call.

If you are unable to pronounce the last name, ask the caller how to pronounce it. The best way to do this is to say, "Who am I speaking with?" If the caller answer with their first name only, use that name to inquire, "How is your last name pronounced?" Once they tell you, use their surname unless instructed by them to use their first name. Again, it's all about respect.

Thank You for Calling

Saying, "thank you" goes a long way in establishing a communicative bond with the customer. Your first "thank you," should be when you answer or connect to the call, "Thank you for calling ABC Company, how *may* I assist you?"

It's my belief that one can never say "thank you" too many times. This is subjective, of course. I believe saying, *"thank you,"* routinely during the call is a sign of respect. Each time you ask the caller for a direct request, and they grant it, say "thank you."

Example:

You: Mr. Jones, please confirm your address for our records.
Mr. Jones: 12345 Rose Map Street, Anyhere, USA 91122
You: Thank you, Mr. Jones. Please confirm your account number.
Mr. Jones: 12345-67
You: Thank you, Mr. Jones.

Some may feel "thank you" was said too many times. Mr. Jones won't feel that way. He will feel attended to and appreciated.

End the call the same way you started it, "Thank you, (*Surname*) for calling ABC Company." This shows the customer that the company values their business and loyalty.

THANK YOU FOR HOLDING

"Thank you for holding," is a phrase you cannot overuse. Most customers hate to be put on hold for any amount of time. Remember, customer service is about servicing the customer. Placing a customer on hold, makes them feel unserved. Thanking for holding shows appreciation for the wait and soothes the bothered customer. It makes them feel the service was uninterrupted.

Customer calls may not be straightforward and answerable by looking on a screen for information or reading the *word track/script*. It *may* take a little more time and light detective work to reconcile the issue. You may need to include your supervisor. In these instances, asking the customer to hold or if they prefer to call back while you research their issue comes into play.

If the customer agrees to a hold, thank them then for holding. Return to the call after a minute or so with, "thank you for holding, we're still researching," or "thank you for holding, here is what I learned." Either way, "thank you for holding," must be the first thing said.

Until the problem is resolved to the customer's satisfaction, the above steps may be repeated, as long as "thank you for holding," is included.

Have a Great Day

Words have power and something as simple as "have a great day," can be the best thing a person has heard all week. A relatively simple phrase, "have a great day," reveals humanity, humility and care.

When you finish a service call, wish the customer a great day. It may make the customer feel that the company cares about them as a person and the kind of day they should have.

Ending a call with, "have a great day," may put a smile on the customer's face and turn their bad day into a good day. Remember, the *power of your smile*, so make sure you smile when you say it!

YOUR ATTITUDE

Attitude is a mental state of being that can make or break your career path. Your attitude is crucial to landing a job, staying employed and moving up the ranks within the job.

In customer service, you are expected to interact with the public which means your attitude must be receptive. Employers want to hire applicants who have good attitudes. Employers do not want employees who can not get along with others, display bad attitudes with eyerolls and speak in harsh tones. Employers do not want employees who refuse to take direction or take direction with overwhelming pushback.

If someone has told you or you feel you have a bad attitude, conduct a self-evaluation every morning before going to work for a week. This will help you be aware of what you need to work on. We all need self-work on something. Every morning ask yourself, "Is my attitude":

- Trainable?
- Humble?
- Grateful?
- Respectful?
- Thankful?

- Working?
- My Best?

If you answer no to any of the above you may need to adjust your attitude accordingly, Answering no may cause you to:

- Not follow directions
- Not pay attention
- Disagree with everything
- Not get along or work well with others

All of this is setting yourself up for failure on your own accord. You will be monitored very closely by your supervisor and be tagged as a difficult employee. This could lead to termination. So, it's important to have a positive, receptive attitude.

When you work on attitudes that need improvement, your personal outlook on life will improve as well as your personal and professional relationships.

In the end, a positive attitude will make you a better person, more productive and on track for a promotion.

CONTINUOUSLY WORKING ON YOU

POLITENESS & COURTESY

Be considerate of others. Incorporate a blend of politeness and courtesy into your natural personality. When you are thoughtful and willing to help others, it makes you look good. It reveals a person of civility and humility. Good manners. A person considerate of others.

Society tends to overlook courteous people and give much attention to the rude, discourteous and inconsiderate. If you are lacking in the politeness category, identify how you can improve your courteous behavior. I'll tell you a secret, it starts with your *attitude*.

Practice courtesies. Be polite. Notice the difference in your relationships with your co-workers. More thoughtfulness and civility will make you a better employee and co-worker.

Power of "Thank You"

Saying "thank you," is not hard when someone does something nice for you. Saying "thank you" builds relationships, especially on the job. It shows that you have respect for other people. You have manners. You appreciate acts of kindness.

The language of manners builds self-esteem and confidence. Other important phrases to remember:

- Please
- Yes, Please
- No, Thank You

Remembering to use the language of manners allows you to control the dynamic of the communication. It does not matter if the other person doesn't exhibit good manners. Remember, we cannot change the behavior of other people, only our own. You are respecting yourself first!

Saying "thank you" will go a long way in opening job opportunities for you. Tie the power of "thank you" with *Thank You for Calling* and *Thank You for Holding* to better understand why both phrases are so important on the job.

No Judgment Zone

We tend to want to judge others, friends, family and co-workers. Wholesale judgment of others is not an attractive personality trait. It sometimes can reveal insecurities and singlemindedness.

Respect others as they are and not as we want them to be based on our own version of how a person should look, act, or sound. Work on self-improvement and other areas of your life that need improving. Try to minimize, if not erase your judgmental nature while on the job and off.

Be accepting of others who may disagree with you or act different from what you are used to or expect. Keep an open mind when trying to nurture business and personal relationships. Make a habit of listening, complimenting and thanking people.

Be or become a thoughtful person.

Self-Evaluation: You According to You

The next exercises are to help guide you in areas where you may need improvement to assist in your customer service job search. A self-evaluation reveals how you can improve in:

- Problem Solving
- Ability to Listen
- Attentiveness
- Emotional Mindfulness
- Resourcefulness
- Positive Language
- Time Management Skills

Take the time to write down how you can work on these areas. There is space for you to write directly in the book. Grab a pen or pencil.

We all need improvement. It's an ongoing, never-ending process. Be honest with yourself and complete each exercise as best you can. If you can't complete the exercise, return to it to see if you can complete it then. If that happens, you will have proven to yourself you've had some personal growth. I am cheering for you! I know you can do this and become the best customer service representative you can be. The first step was wanting it. The second step was getting this book to learn how to go after it. The third step is going for it! GO GET IT! Go get that job you SO deserve!

Problem Solving

I understand how to offer advice or solve a solution to a problem or concern.

Yes_____ No_____

Write down how you have offered advice or solved a problem in a situation on a job or everyday engagements with people. If no, describe how you can improve problem solving skills.

_____

_____

_____

_____

_____

_____

_____

_____

_____

_____

_____

_____

_____

Ability to Listen

I have the patience to listen to a person's concern before responding.

Yes_____ No_____

Write down how you have used patience in your conversations with people by listening to their concerns before responding. If no, describe how can you become more patient and improve listening skills.

_____

_____

_____

_____

_____

_____

_____

_____

_____

_____

_____

_____

_____

_____

Attentiveness

I pay attention to people. Undivided attention. Mindful of feedback.

Yes_____ No_____

Write down the situations in which you gave someone your full attention although you were not that interested. If no, describe how you can become more attentive.

_____

_____

_____

_____

_____

_____

_____

_____

_____

_____

_____

_____

Emotional Mindfulness

Do you tend to take adverse feedback personally, lash out in a negative manner, or do you brush it off and rise above it? If no, explain why you were not able to brush it off and rise above the perceived offense.

Yes_____ No_____

Give examples of when you were faced with adverse criticism and did not take it personally. Describe the situation and how you counteracted the criticism.

_____

_____

_____

_____

_____

_____

_____

_____

_____

_____

_____

Resourcefulness

Do you do more than what is expected of you when helping people?

Yes_____ No_____

Describe how you have done more than expected in helping people. If no, think about what can be done to improve your helpfulness in situations.

_____

_____

_____

_____

_____

_____

_____

_____

_____

_____

_____

_____

_____

Positive Language

You focus on verbalizing positive language. If not, dig deep and describe how you could incorporate positive language when engaging other people.

Yes_____ No_____

Provide events in which you focused on speaking positively and not negatively. What ways can you modify your attitude of negative thinking and focus on the positive?

_____

_____

_____

_____

_____

_____

_____

_____

_____

_____

_____

Time Management Skills

Do you have the ability to organize time efficiently and get things done in a timely manner without compromising quality tasks?

Yes_____ No_____

Describe how you go about your day and get tasks accomplished with minimal disruption. What ways can you improve management of your time doing routine tasks?

_____

_____

_____

_____

_____

_____

_____

_____

_____

_____

_____

_____

_____

CONCLUSION

I'm going to end with a customer service hiring example of my own. I interviewed a young person a few years out of high school for an office position. I submitted the hiring paperwork to Human Human Resources for review. Human Resources responded with a report and recommendation to not hire the applicant. The report included unpaid library fines that had been reported to the credit bureaus.

What I read into that report was a person who read books. A literate person I could relate to and got to know in an in-person interview. She wanted a job in an office after working as a retail cashier. She wanted to move up in the job market and support her young family.

I hired her because I saw potential and trainability. With determination and a willingness to learn, this employee learned the job protocols, duties and obtained new skills quickly. This employee was promoted to office manager and had been an essential and valued part of my team for over eleven years.

Overall, we all make mistakes in life. We cannot judge a book by its cover or by scrutinizing backstories of candidates, unless it is something of a substantially hazardous nature that would compromise the company or business. No one matriculates through life without a misstep here and there. Forgiveness is grace. We all deserve second and even third chances in life. Don't self-sabotage yourself because of your past. Give yourself the benefit of the doubt and keep knocking on the door to your future.

Our rising generations need opportunities. If no one hires the new job hunter out of high school without prior experience, how can that new job hunter obtain experience? All the many vetting tiers applied by the screener of applications can be worrisome and defeating. That's why I wrote this book. To help the high school graduate and the less desirable applicant become the new hire in a field where the requirements are varied and broad depending on the job. Customer service is one of the fastest growing segments of the job market.

People who WANT to work, DESERVE an opportunity to be hired and earn a living. We live in an imperfect world with imperfect people. Recruiters, interviewers, and companies alike need to stop moving the goal post for entry level positions. Discouraging the high school graduate or anyone with limited education the opportunity to obtain an entry level position is unhealthy competitiveness and offers less empowerment towards the workforce.

Printed in the United States
by Baker & Taylor Publisher Services